Everyday Inventions

CONTENTS

NATIONAL GEOGRAPHIC

Hampton-Brown

School Publishing

Words with <u>ir</u>, <u>er</u>, <u>ur</u>

Look at each picture. Read the words.

ur
er
ir

Example:

b<u>ir</u>d

f<u>er</u>n

n<u>ur</u>se

d<u>ir</u>t

c<u>ur</u>l

sh<u>ir</u>t

sk<u>ir</u>t

p<u>ur</u>se

g<u>ir</u>l

High Frequency
Words

| also |
| call |
| fall |
| important |
| story |
| tomorrow |

Key Words

Read the sentences. Match each sentence to one of the pictures.

What Would You Use?

1. Use this to **call** people to say hi and **also** to make plans for **tomorrow** .

2. Use this if you **fall** and scrape yourself.

3. A home with more than one **story** has this.

4. Use this to spread **important** news.

Who do you call?

Phonics Games

NGReach.com

3

Time Savers and Other Helpers

by Felix Quintos

People invent many things. Some things make life better. Others save time.

skyscraper

It takes a long time to walk to the top of a 50-story skyscraper! Which of these things can take you to the top of a skyscraper in less time than you can walk?

elevator

rope

An elevator can! It is quick.

At one time, ropes lifted elevators. An elevator would fall if its ropes broke. The first safe elevator was sold in 1853. A safe elevator would not fall if its ropes broke.

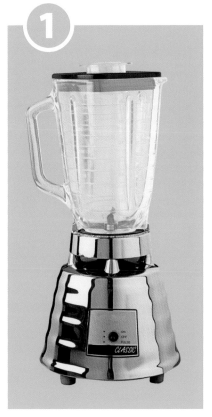

Sometimes thirsty people want a smooth drink. Which of these things can stir and whirl fruit and milk to make a smooth drink?

blender

A blender can! The blender was invented in 1922. Blenders help people to make smooth drinks fast.

Hello!

Which of these things can you use to call someone?

cell phone

purse

You can use a phone! Alexander Graham Bell invented the first phone in 1876. Phones have changed over time. Today many people use cell phones. Now a cell phone can fit in a purse.

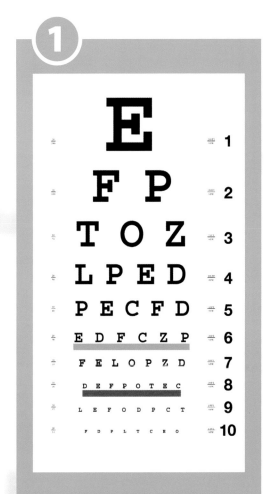

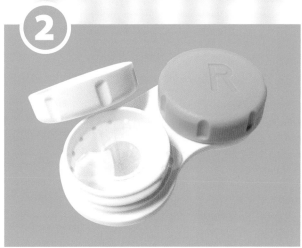

It is important to see well. What may
help you see well if things seem blurry?

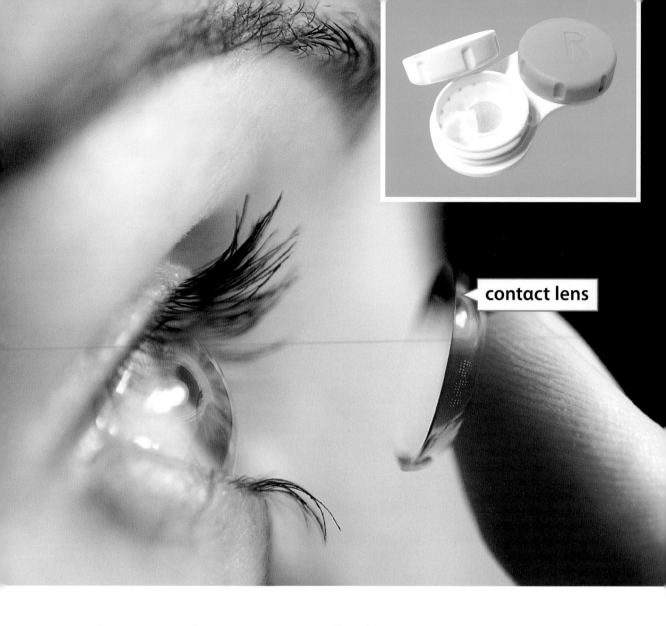

contact lens

Contact lenses may help you to see better! The first contact lenses were made in the 1880s. They were made of hard glass. Now they are made of soft plastic. What might people invent tomorrow? ❖

Words with <u>ir</u>, <u>er</u>, <u>ur</u>

Read these words.

juice	her	blender	slurp	use
whirl	girl	purse	fruit	blurry

Find the words with
ir, **er**, or **ur**. Use
letters to build them.

j u i c e

Talk Together

What can the <u>blender</u> do?

Choose words from the box above
to complete the sentences.

The <u>blender</u> can
<u>whirl</u> the <u>fruit</u>.

Endings -er, -est

Look at each picture. Read the words.

Example:

bigg**er**

bigg**est**

fast**er**

fast**est**

old**est**

long**er**

High Frequency
Words

also
call
fall
important
story
tomorrow

Key Words

Look at the pictures.
Read the sentences.

Skyscraper Trip

1. Gert and Dad go up in a 102-**story** skyscraper.

2. The people who work there do **important** jobs.

3. At the top is a deck, closed in so that people cannot **fall**.

4. Gert tries to **call** out to people far below.

5. **Tomorrow**, Gert and Dad will **also** take a trip.

What do you think Gert and Dad will do tomorrow?

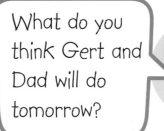

GO! **Phonics Games**

NGReach.com

Stronger, Higher, Quicker, and More!

by Gertrude Fleck

As time passes, people invent new things. They try to make these things be better. Maybe these things are stronger or higher. Or maybe these things work faster.

Stronger Bridges

The oldest bridges are made of stone or wood. Most newer bridges are made of steel. Steel is stronger. Old railway bridges made of wood might fall down.

Many newer bridges are long. One of the longest bridges is almost 24 miles long!

building

Stronger, Higher Buildings

Steel is also used for buildings. Since it's stronger, steel-frame buildings can be higher than stone or wood buildings. The first steel-frame building went up in 1885.

Empire State Building

The Empire State Building is a 102-story skyscraper. People worked to put up this steel-frame building from 1930 to 1931. For a long time, it was the highest skyscraper.

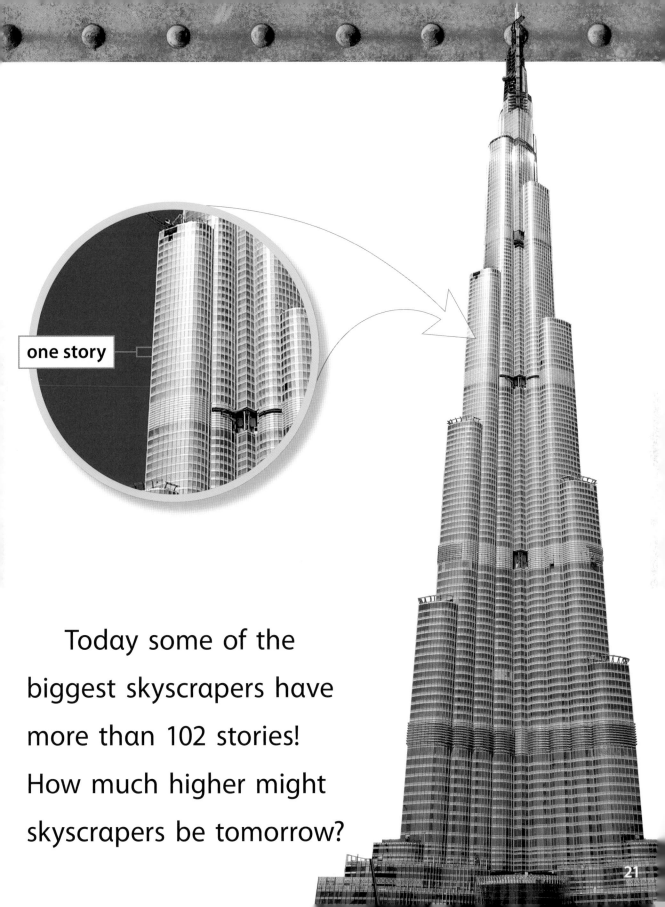

one story

Today some of the biggest skyscrapers have more than 102 stories! How much higher might skyscrapers be tomorrow?

Faster Ways to Reach Out

People have invented many ways to talk to someone far away. You can write and mail a letter. You can call on the phone. That's a faster way.

One of the fastest ways to reach out
to lots of people at once is to use e-mail.
Write your letter on-screen, hit *send*, and
WHOOSH! Your e-mail flies through space
to all your e-mail buddies.

People invent new things all the time. They are always trying to think of ways to make things that are stronger, higher, or faster. What will they invent tomorrow? ❖

Endings -<u>er</u>, -<u>est</u>

Read these words.

higher	longest	skyscraper	trains	horse
railway	fastest	faster	longer	highest

Find the words with the endings
-**er** or -**est**. Use letters
to build them.

h i g h e r

Talk Together

Choose words from the
box above to compare
the things in the pictures.

> One _skyscraper_ is _higher_
> than the others. It is the
> _highest_ _skyscraper_.

25

Look Inside the Skyscraper

Look at the picture with a partner. Take turns reading clues and pointing to answers.

1. Find the third story of the skyscraper.
2. Find the girl with the longest curls.
3. Find a bird perched on a fern.
4. Also find the biggest dog.
5. Find an older man making an important call.
6. Find a ladder that looks like it will fall.

Acknowledgments

Grateful acknowledgment is given to the authors, artists, photographers, museums, publishers, and agents for permission to reprint copyrighted material. Every effort has been made to secure the appropriate permission. If any omissions have been made or if corrections are required, please contact the Publisher.

Photographic Credits

CVR (Cover) contour99/iStockphoto. **2** (bl) graham s. klotz/Shutterstock. (br) Debi Bishop/iStockphoto. (cl) Yuri Arcurs/Shutterstock. (tl) Corel. (tr) PhotoDisc/Getty Images. **3** (b) Liz Garza Williams/Hampton-Brown/National Geographic School Publishing. (tc) Matjaz Boncina/iStockphoto. (tl) Duncan Walker/iStockphoto. (tr) blackred/iStockphoto. **4** KingWu/iStockphoto. **5** (bl) PhotoDisc/Getty Images. (br) fotomak/Shutterstock. (tl) Michael Newman/PhotoEdit. (tr) Stephen Orsillo/Shutterstock. **6** (l) Blend Images/Alamy Images. (r) The Granger Collection, New York. **7** (br) Olinchuk/Shutterstock. (c) Alexandra Draghici/iStockphoto. (tl) Artville. (tr) Stockbyte/Getty Images. **8** Camille Renk - Camille's Kitchen/Getty Images. **9** (b) nyasha/Shutterstock. (l) Stuart Gregory/Getty Images. (r) David Gunn/iStockphoto. **10** (l) Keith Haig/iStockphoto. (r) Stephen Coburn/Shutterstock. **11** (b) Artville. (l) Jeremy Sale/iStockphoto. (r) Steven Wolf/iStockphoto. **12** (bg) John Christian Lonningdal/iStockphoto. (inset) John Christian Lonningdal/iStockphoto. **13** (bl) Liz Garza Williams/Hampton-Brown/National Geographic School Publishing. (br) George Doyle/Jupiterimages. (t) Liz Garza Williams/Hampton-Brown/National Geographic School Publishing. **14** (bl) David Young-Wolff/PhotoEdit. (br) Stephen Frink/Jupiterimages. (cl) Anna Omelchenko/iStockphoto. (cr) fotoIE/iStockphoto. (tl) Kevin Russ/iStockphoto. (tr) imagewerks/Getty Images. **15** (b) Liz Garza Williams/Hampton-Brown/National Geographic School Publishing. (tl) Lya Cattel/iStockphoto. (tr) Russell Kord/Alamy Images. **16** (fg) issad/iStockphoto. (t-border) Dan Roundhill/iStockphoto. (tl) Kerstin Klaassen/iStockphoto. (tr) Kerstin Klaassen/iStockphoto. **16-17** (bg) Bridget McGill/iStockphoto. **17** (inset) Sergey Korotkov/iStockphoto. **18** David Frazier/Corbis. **18-19** (t-border) Dan Roundhill/iStockphoto. **19** calvio/iStockphoto. **20** Joshua Haviv/iStockphoto. **20-21** (t-border) Dan Roundhill/iStockphoto. **21** (inset) feraru nicolae/iStockphoto. (r) feraru nicolae/iStockphoto. **22** (bg) FineCollection/iStockphoto. (inset) Big Cheese Photo/Jupiterimages. **22-23** (t-border) Dan Roundhill/iStockphoto. **23** bonnie jacobs/iStockphoto. **24** Nikada/iStockphoto. (t-border) Dan Roundhill/iStockphoto. **25** (bl) John Foxx Images/Imagestate. (br) Zuzule/Shutterstock. (t) Liz Garza Williams/Hampton-Brown/National Geographic School Publishing.

Illustrator Credits

26-27 Lizzy Rockwell

The National Geographic Society

John M. Fahey, Jr., President & Chief Executive Officer
Gilbert M. Grosvenor, Chairman of the Board

National Geographic School Publishing
Hampton-Brown
www.NGSP.com

Printed in the USA.
Quad Graphics, Leominster, MA

ISBN: 978-0-7362-8048-8

18 19
10 9 8 7 6

also
call
fall
important
story
tomorrow

Target Sound/Spellings

r-Controlled Vowels ir, er, ur	Endings -er, -est
Selection: **Time Savers and Other Helpers**	**Selection:** **Stronger, Higher, Quicker, and More!**
better	biggest
blender(s)	faster
blurry	fastest
first	higher
helpers	highest
over	longest
purse	newer
savers	oldest
skyscraper	quicker
thirsty	stronger
whirl	